GOVERNMENT CONTRACTING: IS IT FOR YOU?

A BEGINNER'S GUIDE TO UNDERSTANDING GOVERNMENT CONTRACTS AND DECIDING IF YOUR BUSINESS HAS WHAT IT TAKES.

PREPARED FOR

Business Owners

PREPARED BY

Kesha L. Murry-Stowe

ISBN: 979-8-9906866-3-2 (Paperback)
         979-8-9906866-4-9 (eBook)

Printed in the United States of America.

First printing, 2024.

Dawn of a New Day 365, LLC
P.O. BOX 384
Grovetown, GA 30813
www.dawnofanewday365.com

Dedication

To the brave small businesses standing at the crossroads of opportunity and uncertainty:

May this book be your trusted compass, guiding you through the maze of government contracting. May you find clarity amidst the codes, conquer the paperwork peaks, and discover whether the treasure of opportunity is worth the quest.

Embark on this adventure with patience, humor, and determination. May your journey be as rewarding as the destination!

Table of Contents

Foreword

Kesha Murry-Stowe, my sister (one the U.S. Army issued to me back in 2003), has authored this incredible book out of her passion for helping people understand the world of government contracting. Before I even cracked it open, I knew it was going to be a great read—because that's just who Kesha is and how she operates. Let me tell you, this book does not disappoint!

I'll never forget when I first met Kesha. It was mid-March, and I was picking up this California girl from the airport in Korea. She steps off the plane in flip-flops, no jacket, completely unfazed by the fact that it was still winter. That's Kesha for you—always bringing her own style and energy to every situation. As you dive into this book, you'll get a glimpse of that same confidence. It feels like she's speaking directly to you—and she is. Kesha has a genuine desire to help those looking to enter the government contracting world, and she firmly believes in sharing her knowledge and lessons learned.

Throughout her time in the U.S. Army, Kesha has demonstrated a level of knowledge and diligence that sets her apart from her peers, and you'll see those attributes reflected in these pages. She's spent over 20 years working in finance and acquisition, first as an enlisted soldier and later as an officer. Her experience laid the foundation for the contracting expert she is today.

In 2008, Kesha made the jump from the Finance Corps to the Acquisition Corps, and I followed her in 2010. Since then, we've both been knee-deep in government contracting—me in the Regular Army, and Kesha in a mix of the Regular Army, Army National Guard, public sector, and private sector. Her ability to see contracting from four different perspectives has given her a unique insight into the field, and that's exactly what makes her the perfect guide for you.

This book is more than just a how-to manual—it's a roadmap for partnering with the U.S. Government and growing your business. If you take Kesha's advice to heart, you'll be on your way to a win-win partnership. Enjoy the ride (you can even wear flip-flops) and enjoy this book. I know I did!

Dawn Daniels
Lieutenant Colonel (Ret.), U.S. Army
Contracting Officer, Army Contracting Command & U.S. Army Corps of Engineers

Preface

If you're holding this book, you might be wondering if the government contracting world has a place for you. Well, I'm here to help you figure that out by telling you about it from an insider's perspective.

For over 15 years, I've been that person poring over lists of potential companies, trying to find the right fit for government projects. I was baffled because I kept seeing the same companies pop up over and over. It got me thinking: there are tons of businesses out there —yours could be one of them—so why were they not showing up on my radar? Well, turns out a lot of entrepreneurs either don't even know that government contracting is a thing or are afraid to step in the water.

Whenever I talked to business owners about stepping into this arena, I got a heap of doubts and misconceptions thrown at me. "That's only for the big guns like Boeing or Lockheed Martin," some would say. Or the classic, "The government won't hire us; we don't have what it takes." Sound familiar? What they needed was someone who would patiently walk them through the process, so they could understand it better.

This book speaks of my passion; it's my labor of love. I've been sent on a mission to dispel the myths concerning government contracting, specifically federal government contracting, while encouraging businesses (especially small businesses) to check out this venture. The door is wide open and there's room for everyone.

I wrote this guide to help you decide if now is the time to embark on this journey.

Acknowledgments

First and foremost, I give honor and glory to God. Thank you, Lord! This book would not have been possible without His strategy, the resources He provided, and the opportunity to enter a new career field 15 years ago that helped me discover a passion and part of my purpose.

My children, James & Amani: Thank you! I appreciate your love and patience. I know my career (and ambitions) has taken us across the globe, and we've had to leave family and friends behind more times than we wanted, know that I see you both. I admire your resilience. I thank God for you guys; this journey would've been lonely without you. I love you both to life!

Family and Friends: Thank you (my tribe, sister circle and community) for believing in me, even when I didn't believe in myself. "Y'all" got on my nerves, so I figured I had better get to work to get "y'all" off my nerves. I appreciate your love and support over the years as I slowly dragged this out.

Peers: I thank God for you all. My journey, passion and vast knowledge concerning government contracting came from our conversations about thresholds, timelines for publicizing requirements, which clauses to incorporate, and when or why justifications were necessary. You helped me become the expert I am.

My editor, Will: You were a Godsend! Thank you so much for your willingness, patience, and kindness. I appreciate you being a part of my publishing team.

My publisher, Dawn: Battleeeee! Thank you for your guidance throughout this process. Your support and breakdown of the whole "authorship" arena made this effort easy to tackle. A sister for life!

Special thanks to COL James Robinson: Sir, your confidence in me as a young contracting professional allowed me room to grow. Thank you for your mentorship and for showing me what true leadership looks like, even in the face of adversity. Although I asked (and still do ask) 1,000 questions, lol, know that I've grown exponentially under your tutelage. I'm a better leader, professional, and person having known you!

Introduction

Welcome, I'm Kesha, a certified government contracting professional, here to serve as your guide on this journey. Just imagine we're having a chat over tea (or coffee, or water).

Let's dive into the world of government contracting, or GovCon. GovCon can also refer to "government contractor". Throughout this book, it will be used to refer to the process.

This guide is your compass in the vast sea of GovCon. It's written for you, the business owner, who's standing at the crossroads probably wondering if the path of GovCon is the right one to take. Whether you run a small local business or a burgeoning enterprise, this book aims to demystify the complex world of GovCon, breaking it down into digestible, manageable pieces.

Our purpose here is threefold: educate, empower, and expand. We'll start by peeling back the layers of what GovCon is. This market is not just for big defense contractors. Actually, any company that can cater to the growing needs of government agencies should continue reading.

As you read, you'll gain insight into how to navigate the bidding process, understand compliance requirements, and manage the unique challenges and opportunities of working with the government. This book isn't just about getting your foot in the door; it's about opening that door wide enough to expand your business' horizons.

But here's the catch - GovCon isn't for everyone. Once the excitement departs, a world filled with different business rules, lots of compliance requirements, and statutory obligations intimidate many business owners. That's why, beyond just educating and guiding, this book challenges you to think critically. Is GovCon the right move for your business? What does it take to succeed in this arena? And most importantly, is the potential reward worth the inherent risks and investments?

With tons of information out there, it can be overwhelming. Here, we aim to cut through the noise, offering a clear and concise overview without skipping nitty-gritty details that are crucial for informed decision-making.

GovCon is this huge, slightly complex, but very interesting field where businesses get to work directly with the government. Instead of hitting the local store and buying things with cash or a debit card, government agencies also shop for products and services by reaching out to businesses through solicitations.

For business owners, GovCon is a big deal. "Why?", because the federal government has over 400 agencies and spends hundreds of billions of dollars annually on contracts, this means there are thousands of opportunities. Compare it to going inside a new store (one you've never been to before), and it has everything you want, need, imagine, and more. Well, the opportunities are much like that, lol. The government needs everything from paper clips to rocket ships, and if your business can provide something they need, you could be in for steady work, which means steady contracts.

We're going to unravel the GovCon puzzle. Our goals are straightforward:

1. Understand the basics of GovCon – what, why, and how.
2. Explore its significance for businesses, especially for entrepreneurs looking to expand their horizons.
3. Navigate through the process of landing a government contract, which can be a game-changer for many businesses.
4. Provide tools to help you assess whether this venture is worth your time.

There's an innovative feature, QR code, placed at the end of some chapters. As you delve into the complexities and opportunities of GovCon these QR codes offer you instant access to exclusive videos where I share additional tips and insights. These videos are another valuable resource to help guide your journey in GovCon.

By the end of this book, you won't just have a thorough understanding of GovCon; you'll be equipped to assess whether this path aligns with your business goals and capabilities. You'll have a clearer picture of how GovCon works and how it can be a potential goldmine for your business. You'll also get the hang of some lingo, processes, and strategies that make successful government contractors stand out. Who knows, it maybe your map to a treasure chest in the vast ocean of government spending.

Remember, this guide is not about winning a contract; it's about understanding if this competitive and complex market is a suitable and sustainable avenue for your business' growth. So, to find out if you have what it takes, turn the page and keep reading. I'm excited to see where the tides take you in your entrepreneurial journey. -Proverbs 3:5-6; "Trust in the LORD with all your heart and lean not on your own understanding; in all your ways submit to him, and he will make your paths straight." (NIV, Bible)

Chapter 1

WHAT IS GOVERNMENT CONTRACTING? (GOVCON)

Imagine you're throwing a massive party, but you don't have everything you need, like food, decorations, and maybe a DJ. What do you do? You go out and find the right people who can supply you with these things. That's essentially what GovCon is– the way government agencies purchase things they can't get among themselves.

For the party, some items can be purchased at the local store, while other items, like facility and equipment rentals might involve contracts. Contracts are formal; they outline the responsibilities of all parties, especially Buyers and Sellers. In federal government contracting, federal agencies are the buyers.

Agencies put out detailed lists of what they need to the public, known as solicitations. Solicitations are published in one of three ways, request for quote (RFQ), request for proposal (RFP), or invitation to bid (IFB). This ensures fairness and encourages competition as much as possible (as much as possible because this isn't always the case).

The scope of what agencies need can be wild (far out there sometime, like, Zombie Apocalypse Training; yep, I said what you think I said, lol). Agencies buy more than just paper, pencils, and janitorial services; we're talking about everything from building spaceships to providing security, or even running entire cafeterias. If you can name it, the government probably needs it at some point.

When the government puts out the word that they need something, businesses from all over can throw their hat in the ring. Businesses prepare proposals that say, "Here's what we can do for you, and here's what it'll cost." The government then sifts through all of the proposals, checks out who meets all the requirements, who's most reliable, and who's offering the best deal.

Contrary to popular belief, contracting professionals aren't just looking at the price tag. The government must consider various things, like whether the business can handle the job, if the business is responsible, and the business' reputation concerning its employees and the environment. Plus, there's a bunch of laws and regulations to follow, which contribute to a fair process.

Once all the i's are dotted and the t's crossed, the government picks a winner, and bam, you've got yourself a government contract. In a nutshell, it's how agencies make sure they're spending taxpayer dollars wisely and getting what they need to help keep the big machine (the federal government) running smoothly.

Importance of GovCon in the Economy
Ready to hear about the world of government contracting, and its impact on the economy, from a Contracting Officer's perspective? You still got your tea, coffee, or water? If you don't, grab it or get a refill cause we're just starting.

GovCon is a bit of a powerhouse in the economic world (for those that know). It's huge and plays a vital role in both the national and local economies. The federal government is the largest customer in the world, buying everything from office supplies to high-tech defense equipment. A large machine such as this spends more than a few dollars.

Let's talk numbers to paint a clearer picture. In recent years, the U.S. government has been spending upwards of $500 billion annually on contracts. These contracts are spread across various sectors – defense, healthcare, education, infrastructure (construction and information technology-IT), etc. This diversity means there are opportunities for all kinds of businesses, big and small.

What's interesting about GovCon is its impact. Nationally, government contracts can serve as a driver of innovation. Government contracts can lead to new research and development, pushing industries forward. Locally, when a company in your community wins a government contract, they not only benefit, but the whole area may benefit. It can mean more jobs, better local services, and a stronger local economy.

One of the most appealing aspects of GovCon for businesses is its stability, especially in volatile industries like IT, energy, and heatlhcare. Unlike the commercial market, where demand can fluctuate wildly, government needs are consistent. They always need something, and they're legally obligated to pay their bills on time. This consistency makes government contracts a relatively stable source of income, which is important, especially in uncertain economic times.

For businesses, this stability translates to predictability in revenue streams. It allows for better long-term planning and investing. Whether you're supplying everyday items or specialized services, if you can meet the government's needs, you could have a reliable, long-term customer.

Summary
GovCon isn't just a procurement process; it's a significant driver of both national and local economic health. For businesses, it offers a range of opportunities and a level of stability that's hard to find elsewhere. Understanding and tapping into this market can be a game-changer, making GovCon an avenue worth exploring for businesses looking to expand and solidify their presence in a competitive market.

Manifest
Inc.

Please scan the QR code for more insight. If you would like to further the conversation, feel free to reach out via Facebook, Instagram, or schedule a call via our "Lean on Me" service.

Chapter 2

THE REWARDS OF GOVCON

The Reliability of Uncle Sam – Your Steadiest Client

Imagine running a business as you juggle cash flow to ensure the lights stay on, and boom — the economy decides to take a wild ride (think COVID-19). Scary, right? If you're in the GovCon game, you've got a client who's pretty much as reliable as your favorite old truck. The government isn't going to ghost you when times get tough. They're the kind of customer who pays, even when the economy's playing hardball.

With GovCon, in addition to securing a steady client, having a federal government agency as a customer brings clout and credibility to your business. I've seen how having the government as a client serves as a powerful tool in your marketing arsenal and a friend in your financial corner.

Another great aspect of GovCon is its power to supercharge your business' growth. Landing a government contract can cause a growth spurt in your business journey.

1. When the Economy Sneezes, GovCon Doesn't Catch a Cold

Economic downturns can wreak havoc on your business journey. But here's a secret: When you're working with federal contracts, you're working with a client that doesn't back out quickly. Federal agencies attempt to work with their contractors through periods of economic instability.

How is that? The federal government receives appropriated funds (funds given for a specific purpose). The President's budget approved by Congress provides this funding (A.K.A money). Funds are used for agencies to operate (pay payroll, pay rent and utilities, etc.), run programs, and enter contracts to purchase products or services. So, if you have a contract and deliver products or services as promised, you can count on your invoices being paid. It's not magic; it's just good business.

2. The Long Haul: Contracts That Stick Around

Federal agencies enter contracts for various reasons, and the reason determines the length of the contract. Most contracts for services are at least a year long, and many extend beyond that with options for renewal.

This isn't just about having work; it's about having predictable, consistent work. GovCon can be the difference between your business operating invoice to invoice and generating steady revenue. With longer contracts, you can plan for the future, invest into your business, and maybe even splurge on that fancy coffee machine for the office.

3. The Prestige Factor: Winning Where It's Tough

Securing a government contract is like getting on of the most coveted stamps of approval. Why? Because everyone knows it's not a walk in the park. The process is rigorous, the competition is fierce, and the standards are sky-high. So, when you tell the world, "We've won a government contract.", that's a big deal.

This seal of approval is golden for your marketing. It tells potential clients, "We play in the big leagues." With successful contract performance, your business gains credibility. It can set you apart in the private sector, where the perception that you've passed the stringent requirements of the federal government can make your business more attractive.

4. Contracts as Collateral: Financial Flexibility

Did you know that your government contract can be more than a source of revenue? It can also be a key to unlocking financial opportunities. Banks and lenders loan to businesses showing stability with guaranteed income; and what's more stable than a contract with the biggest spender in the world? Your government contract can be used as collateral when you're looking to get a loan or line of credit (Assignment of Claims). This means you can use your contract to grow your business, invest in new ventures, or smooth out cash flow wrinkles. Lenders are more willing to listen when they know you've got reliable government-backed income.

5. The School of Hard Knocks: Upping Your Game with Standards

Landing a government contract is exciting, it also means your business is about to get a serious workout. The government has a reputation for being a stickler about rules and standards, and for good reasons because federal agencies must ensure good stewardship of taxpayer dollars. Whether industry-specific regulations or broader government standards, these rules are akin to a high bar set for a jumper – they challenge you to leap higher.

Compliance might seem like a tough nut to crack, but it's actually your secret weapon for growth. It nudges your business to adopt cutting-edge practices, be it in quality management, cybersecurity, or environmental responsibility. You're not just checking boxes for the sake of a contract; you're building a robust framework that can transform your operations from the ground up.

6. Quality Control: Not Just a Buzzword

In the GovCon world, quality control plans are necessary. Developing and maintaining rigorous quality control procedures ingrain a culture of excellence in your team and can instill confidence in your government client(s).

This journey towards enhanced quality control can set a new standard for every project you undertake, government or otherwise. The discipline and precision you develop spill over into every aspect of your business. Your team lives by these standards, your clients notice and before you know it, your business' reputation gets more shine.

7. The Ripple Effect: Beyond the Contract

Here's the thing: the rewards of a government contract extend way beyond the lifespan of the contract itself. The experience, reputation, and operational standards you develop under a government contract become a part of your business' DNA. They increase your business' resilience, credibility, and competitiveness.

With each government project you successfully complete, your business grows in size and in stature. You become part of an elite club that has stood up to the scrutiny of one of the toughest clients out there – the federal government.

Summary

As we close this chapter, remember that a government contract is more than a revenue stream; it's a growth engine. It propels your business to adopt industry best practices, fosters a culture of quality, and elevates your standing in the marketplace. It's a journey of transformation that not only prepares your business to meet the challenges of today, but to embrace the opportunities of tomorrow. Now, that's what I call a winning proposition!

Manifest Inc.

Please scan the QR code for more insight. If you would like to further the conversation, feel free to reach out via Facebook, Instagram, or schedule a call via our "Lean on Me" service.

Chapter 3
THE CHALLENGES OF GOVCON

A Closer Look at Government Agencies as Clients
As someone who's been in the trenches of GovCon, I've seen many bright-eyed businesses enter the fray, overwhelmed by the sheer volume of information and complexity involved. While an earlier chapter illuminated rewards and opportunities in GovCon, it's only fair to explore the other side of the coin—challenges and quirks that come with having government agencies as clients. GovCon is a complex, often convoluted world, layered with unique challenges and hurdles.

1. Understanding the Layered Process
Government contracting is far from a monolithic process. The layered, multifaceted beast adds complexity with each layer of the process. Why? Because unlike private sector, where a contract might be as straightforward as supply and demand, GovCon is woven by fabrics of public accountability, regulatory compliance, and needs of diverse agencies.

It's crucial to recognize that no two solicitations are identical. There's no cookie-cutter requirement. Every requirement is a unique snowflake, shaped by specific needs of agencies and the end-users they serve. So as a contractor, your approach can't be one-size-fits-all. Each response (quote, proposal, or bid) must be tailored, meticulously crafted to align with requirements in solicitations.

Tailoring approaches for each unique requirement can be time-consuming and resource intensive. The intricacy of each solicitation demands thorough research, meticulous planning, and an understanding of specific agency needs and operational language.

2. The Proliferation of Agencies

Government contracting involves a mosaic of agencies, each with its own culture, priorities, and operational frameworks. Navigating this landscape is like navigating a complex archipelago, where each island (agency) has its own rules and customs. For contractors, this means understanding specific requirements of a project and the modus operandi (M.O.) of the agency.

Why the variation? The federal government is a large organized system with hundreds of interconnected agencies. Each agency represents something different and supports a different mission. The Department of Defense (DoD), for instance, operates in a markedly different terrain than, the Department of Education (ED). Their needs, priorities, and operational frameworks differ, and so do their contracting requirements. This diversity is reflected in the solicitations they issue.

3. Varying Authors of Solicitations

The fact that solicitations are penned by various contracting professionals adds to the complexities. Contracting professionals are as varied as the agencies they represent. Each professional has their unique style, use of discretion, and set of expectations. What might be a straightforward process with one contracting professional could turn into a labyrinth with another. This inconsistency can be bewildering, often requiring contractors to be chameleons, constantly adapting to the differing styles and expectations of each professional. This diversity, while a testament to the human element in government operations, provides insight into the complexities of the contracting process.

4. The Challenges of the Process

If there's one word to describe GovCon, it's meticulous. Every step, from solicitation to contract award, is governed by stringent regulations and procedures. This meticulousness ensures fairness and accountability, but also translates into a slow, often cumbersome process.

-The Snail's Pace: Government contracting isn't for the impatient. The process is laden with procedural checkpoints, each adding time to the clock. It can be frustrating, especially when resources are tied up waiting for a decision that seems to perpetually linger on the horizon.

-The Red Tape: The regulatory framework surrounding government contracts is dense and daunting. Staying compliant isn't merely about adhering to the letter of the law; it's about navigating an intricate web of regulations that touch upon every facet of the contracting process.

-The Cost of Customization: The uniqueness of each requirement means responses must be customized. Constant customization can cause creative and financial challenges. The effort and resources invested in crafting these made-to-order proposals may be significant, with no guaranteed return on investment.

5. Speaking Governmentese: The Language of Government Contracting
Imagine walking into a party where everyone's speaking a language you've never heard before, that's what stepping into the world of GovCon feels like for the inexperienced. You learn a different business language. A language filled with acronyms, jargon, and terms that can make anyone's head spin. Here's a taste of what you're up against:

-BPA, PO, IDIQ, Oh My!: BPA (Blanket Purchase Agreement), PO (Purchase Order), and IDIQ (Indefinite Delivery, Indefinite Quantity) are the tips of the iceberg. Each term stands for a different method of procurement, each with rules, expectations, and procedures. Potential contractors must understand what they stand for and how to navigate each process effectively.

-The Jargon Jungle: Terms like cost-reimbursable (CR), fixed-price (FP), and GSA (General Services Administration) Schedules are part of the daily vernacular. Each term carries significant implications for how you bid, how you manage contracts, and how you get paid.

6. The Fire Hydrant of Information

It's not just a stream of information; it's a torrent. From foreign acronyms to dense regulations that can rival War and Peace in length, the learning curve is steep; almost vertical. The initial phase of entering GovCon involves a steep learning curve. Misunderstanding a term or failing to grasp a regulation can lead to compliance issues, rejected proposals, or even legal problems. For small businesses or newcomers, the sheer volume of information and the complexity of processes can be daunting, making the barrier to entry feel insurmountable.

Overcoming Challenges

Government contracting is a business opportunity and a partnership with one of the most steadfast entities out there. Federal government contracts can provide a chance to weather economic storms with confidence and plan with some assurance. Having the federal government as a client drives your business to adopt industry best practices, fosters a culture of quality, and elevates your standing in the marketplace. It's a journey of transformation that prepares you to meet the challenges of today, while embracing the opportunities of tomorrow.

Despite the challenges, GovCon remains an attractive prospect for many. Why? Because of the rewards- financially, skillfully, and socially. The key is to approach it with eyes wide open, understand the challenges and prepare accordingly.

Summary

Although the opportunities of GovCon can be rewarding, the complexity is undeniable. Every contract is unique, requiring tailored approaches for each agency, all of which operate with their own rules and cultures. The process can be slow, packed with regulations, and full of confusing jargon. Customization is costly, and navigating the mountain of information can feel overwhelming, especially for newcomers. However, with the right preparation and understanding of these challenges, the rewards of GovCon may still make it a worthwhile pursuit.

Manifest
Inc.

Please scan the QR code for more insight. If you would like to further the conversation, feel free to reach out via Facebook, Instagram, or schedule a call via our "Lean on Me" service.

Chapter 4
THE GOVCON PROCESS

Are you ready to navigate the intricate maze of GovCon? It's a world filled with opportunities and, yes, quite a bit of paperwork. But fear not! As a seasoned Contracting Officer, I'm here to guide you through the twists and turns. Let's break down this journey into three main phases: pre-award, award, and post-award. We'll journey through each phase identifying applicable tasks for you as a government contractor.

Pre-Award Phase: Getting Your Ducks in a Row
Picture the pre-award phase as prep time. During this phase, you'll learn to understand the lay of the land and position your business as a worthy contender. Here's where you find out what government agencies really want and how you can tailor the products and/or services you provide to meet those needs.

Let's talk about understanding requirements. When an agency issues an RFQ or RFP, they're issuing more than a document; it's a wishlist of what they need to accomplish their mission. Your job? Decode that wishlist and figure out how your business can deliver the "goods".

Agencies do market research to find potential suppliers, and so should you. Learn your competitors, price products and services smartly, and showcase what sets you apart. Government contracting isn't about being the best; it's about being the best fit for what the agency needs.

-Market Research and Registration: Before anything else, you need to understand the market. What do government agencies need? Are your products or services a fit? Use resources like SAM.gov, Unison Marketplace, and FedConnect to find out what contracts are out there. Make sure your business is registered in the System for Award

Management (SAM). This is a must when bidding on government contracts.

-Understanding Solicitations: When you find potential contract opportunities, read all solicitation documents carefully. This includes attachments, exhibits, and instructions for bidding (see Instructions to Offerors, or something that resembles this wording). Pay attention to the Statement of Work (SOW) or Performance Work Statement (PWS), which identifies the agency's problem and outlines the requirement.

Let's not overlook the importance of crafting a compelling proposal. This phase is your chance to shine and persuade the agency that choosing your business isn't just a safe bet, but the best bet. Make every page of your proposal count, highlight how your products and services align with their requirements, and back it up with solid evidence.

-Preparing Proposals: It's time to put in work. A proposal should clearly explain how you'll meet the government's needs, by stating your solution to the problem, how you plan to implement the solution to meet requirements, at what cost, and why you're the best choice. Make sure to follow the solicitation's format and submission guidelines. And remember, detail and clarity are your friends.

-Questions and Amendments: Don't hesitate to ask questions if any-thing in the solicitation is unclear. Government agencies usually note a specific time for asking questions in the solicitation. Also, keep an eye out for amendments to the solicitation; they can change crucial details, which may impact your proposal.

Award Phase: Showtime!
This is it—the moment you've been waiting for. You've submitted your proposal, now it's up to the agency to pick a winner. But what happens behind closed doors? Let's shed some light on that.

Evaluation is a meticulous process. Agencies comb through each proposal, weighing factors like your technical solution, price, and past performance. Proposals should aim to exceed requirements.

Once proposals are submitted, they're checked for responsiveness and evaluated against the criteria set out in the solicitation. Evaluation criteria and factors are often listed in the solicitation, usually in Sections L and M. If your proposal is in the competitive range, discussions may take place to negotiate terms, prices, or details of your offer. Be prepared to justify your offered price and explain how you'll deliver on contract requirements.

And then, the award! If your proposal offers the best value, congratulations are in order. Remember, the award is just the beginning; next, deliver on your promises.

Post-Award Phase: Keeping the Ball Rolling
You've won a contract, yet the journey is far from over. The post-award phase is about delivering results and building a relationship with the agency.

Contract administration is your new best friend. You'll be in regular contact with the Contracting Officer and/or the Contracting Officer's Representative (COR), making sure you're on track with contract requirements, schedules, and budgets. Transparency and communication are key. The government will watch and check your performance against the contract's terms (see the Quality Assurance Surveillance Plan- QASP). Proactively address any issues and be sure to document everything. Successful performance can lead to more opportunities. Keep the agency in the loop about your progress, and don't shy away from discussing challenges or seeking guidance.

Audits are possible, so ensure you're complying with all contract stipulations, including labor laws, safety standards, and reporting requirements. Non-compliance can lead to penalties or even contract termination.

Changes may occur in the form of modifications, and how you handle modifications can make or break your success. Maintaining flexibility when performing on contracts helps implement changes without delaying progress. Your ability to adapt and solve problems facilitates success on contracts and opens doors for future opportunities.

Once contract performance ends, contract closeout begins. Make sure to cross your t's and dot your i's by providing all deliverables and settling all invoices. Take this time to reflect on your performance (make sure you're doing this throughout the process as well). Each contract is a learning experience, helping you refine your approach for the next opportunity.

Summary

After walking through these phases, you might be wondering: Is GovCon right for my company? Here's the deal – it's not only about whether you can do the work, but whether you can navigate and manage the contracting process itself. Understanding the phases of GovCon guide you in narrowing your focus on specific tasks at varying times throughout the process.

Although embarking on the GovCon journey can seem daunting, with the right mindset and preparation, it transforms into a path filled with opportunities. Provide solutions you promised in fulfilling agency requirements, stay diligent in your efforts, and never stop learning from each experience. So, gear up, stay the course, and let's make your GovCon adventure a resounding success!

Chapter 5

UNDERSTANDING THRESHOLDS

Dipping your toes into federal contracts also means gaining an understanding of procurement thresholds. Understanding these thresholds helps you focus your attention on methods used to advertise opportunities. Each threshold consists of a set of rules based on dollar limits that govern the procurement process from beginning to end.

Although there are 3 levels mentioned in the FAR (Federal Acquisition Regulation- the manual for federal government contracting), I'm going to discuss 5 because things get murky between the first 2 levels. I promise not to leave you "hanging", so keep reading.

During acquisition planning, it's important for contracting professionals to estimate the cost of requirements. Their estimates determine how agencies solicit opportunities, evaluate offers, award contracts, and manage requirements. Requirements with estimates between $10,000-$250,000 are automatically set aside (reserved) for small businesses. YES, you read correctly!

Before we get deep, I'll briefly discuss the last level (level 3, actually 5 in my head); which is affectionately referred to as "Above SAT". The simplified acquisition threshold (SAT) is $250,000. Products, services, or construction costs exceeding SAT are considered "Above SAT" requirements. Rules dictating how agencies conduct pre-award, award, and post-award tasks can change significantly at this level.

Micro-Purchase Threshold
The micro-purchase threshold (level 1) is a sweet spot for companies looking to start small and dream big. The micro purchase threshold is set at $10,000. What does this mean for you?- If a federal agency needs

to buy products or services under this amount, they can do so without going through a complex bidding process. This is your chance to shine without the red tape!

The process is straight forward: agency buyers can simply use a government purchase card (GPC, it's a credit card) to buy directly from sellers. It's fast, easy, and a great way to start building your reputation with government clients. These opportunities may be found on government agencies' websites and by networking with government buyers (the agency's contracting or small business office can assist with identification of agency buyers).

Within this threshold, agency customers/buyers select vendors to meet their requirements. It's recommended they get at least 3 vendors to submit quotes, but this isn't required. However, government buyers must ensure competition among sellers, so buyers tend to rotate vendors. To position your company for these opportunities, make sure your company is registered in SAM, update your company's profile in the Small Business Administration's (SBA) Dynamic Small Business Search (DSBS) tool, and if possible, create a professional website to make it easier for buyers to find you.

The "Gap" Threshold

Next, level 2 (one I added) covers a gap the FAR doesn't explicitly mention between $10,000.01-$15,000. If a proposed contract is expected to fall within these limits, agencies generally follow the same methods for seeking buyers as stated in level 1. The main difference is that a contract serves as the procurement method instead of a purchase card when buying products or services.

Simplified Acquisition Threshold(SAT) Under $25,000

Level 3 (another one I added) details a threshold between $15,000.01 and $25,000. This range is a step up from micro-purchases and offers greater opportunities while keeping bureaucracy to a minimum.

For contracts within this threshold, the government can use simplified acquisition procedures (SAP). SAP means less paperwork and faster decision times. While there's a bit more competition than micro-purchases, the process is still designed to be less intimidating for small businesses. You won't need to navigate the full-blown bidding process, but you should prepare a simple quote or proposal to put your best foot forward.

Networking and marketing are crucial here. Attending industry days, reaching out to agency small business specialists, and making sure your business is registered in the SAM are all great ways to stay informed. Also, opportunities expected to be within this threshold must be posted in a public place, but not necessarily on SAM. The "public place" can be federal agencies' websites, Unison Marketplace, a bulletin board outside of the contracting office, local newspapers, and/or SAM. Being proactive can set you apart from the crowd, so don't hesitate to visit a federal government contracting office in your area (just make sure you call first).

Simplified Acquisition Threshold(SAT) Under $250,000
Level 4, purchases between $25,000.01 and $250,000 get a bit more competitive, but the opportunities grow exponentially.

This range still falls under SAT (requirements at or under $250,000). Government agencies aim to streamline the procurement process using SAP. However, there are a few more rules to follow. For starters, these contracts require public advertising via a governmentwide point of entry (GPE), which must ultimately lead to SAM. Unless an exception such as using an 8(a) set aside exists, all contract opportunities expected to be within this threshold can and should be found on SAM. This is where your diligent preparation pays off. Ensure your proposals are sharp, pricing competitive, and value propositions clear.

Simplified Acquisitions Procedures (SAP)
What Are Simplified Acquisition Procedures?- In the grand scheme of

GovCon, SAP is like the express lane at your favorite grocery store: designed to be quicker and less complicated than the standard checkout lines (or in our case, procurement processes).

SAP applies to purchases that fall under the SAT. SAP is tailored for small businesses like yours. It's a golden opportunity to step into the GovCon world without getting bogged down by the extensive regulations that larger contracts entail.

The Nitty-Gritty: How SAP Works

Under SAP, the government can obtain quotes rather than formal offers (proposals/bids). If the government posts an RFQ, you won't have to jump through as many hoops. You should still prepare a solid, straightforward quote, showcasing the value and quality of your products or services. Remember, clear and concise is the name of the game.

With SAP, the evaluation process isn't as rigid. Government agencies look for the best value, which doesn't mean the lowest price. Evaluations are based on lowest price technically acceptable (LPTA) specifications or trade-offs and must comply with the factors stated in the solicitation. Contracting Officers don't have to establish a competitive range, enter discussions, nor score offers when using SAP.

Tips for Success

Before I wrap up, here are a few nuggets of wisdom to help you navigate the SAP world; and these are in no set order.

1) Get Certified: As applicable, begin working on small business certifications (woman-owned (WOSB),veteran-owned (VOSB), etc.) via SBA.

2) Market Directly to Agencies: Find out what agencies buy what you sell. Depending on your product or service, there could be a lot, so identify 4-5 agencies to market too. You'll be able to find agency contracting professionals using SAM and Google.

3) Monitor Opportunities Regularly: Set up and save an automated search in SAM. You can set up multiple searches, focusing on specific industries or agencies.

4) Price Competitively: Know your industry. Ensure your prices are competitive while demonstrating value. Agencies appreciate vendors that offer cost-effective solutions, especially in simplified acquisitions.

Summary

Federal procurement thresholds shape the contracting process. From micro-purchases under $10,000 to contracts up to $250,000 under the Simplified Acquisition Threshold (SAT), each level presents unique opportunities for small businesses. Simplified Acquisition Procedures (SAP) streamline the process, making it easier for businesses to compete; therefore, reducing barriers to entry. Embarking on the journey of GovCon can be overwhelming, but understanding these thresholds and procedures is a step toward success.

Manifest
Inc.

Please scan the QR code for more insight. If you would like to further the conversation, feel free to reach out via Facebook, Instagram, or schedule a call via our "Lean on Me" service.

Chapter 6

DECISION-MAKING TOOLS

Before you chart your course towards securing a government contract, it's important to assess whether your small business is ready for the journey ahead. This chapter will provide you with a practical framework or checklist to gauge your readiness. Think of it as your business' life vest, designed to keep you afloat as you navigate these waters.

This chapter is designed to provide you with a straightforward, easy-to-digest framework to assess your readiness for government contracts. I've laid out tasks in checklists, so you can easily track where you stand. Let's make sure you've got everything lined up for success!

Small Business Government Contracting Readiness Checklist

Understanding the Government Marketplace

The government/public market is not your typical commercial market; it's a unique beast with its own rules, regulations, and buying patterns. Here are somethings to help you understand the space better:

Task	Description	Completed (Yes/No)
Research Government Market	Have you researched how and what the government agencies buy goods/services in your industry?	
Market Analysis	Identifying past contracts and understanding the demand for your products or services is key. Use USASpending.gov, search via NAICS.	
Attend Training	Register with SBA and your local APEX (formerly Procurement Technical Assistance Center (PTAC)) to attend training.	

Compliance and Registrations

Make sure your paperwork is in order. Government contracting requires specific registrations and compliance standards:

Task	Description	Completed (Yes/No)
Business Formation	Is your business legally formalized within your state, county or city? Do you have an EIN?	
Regulatory Compliance	Are you familiar with the Federal Acquisition Regulation (FAR) and ready to comply with government contracting laws?	
Understand Set-Asides	Are you familiar with set-aside contracts for small businesses?	

Financial Stability

Before taking on government contracts, assess your financial health:

Task	Description	Completed (Yes/No)
Bank Account	Establish a bank account specifically for your company in your company's name.	
Analyze Cash Flow	Can your business handle delayed payments common in government contracts?	
Secure Financing	Do you have a line of credit or other financing to cover upfront costs?	
Review Accounting System	Is your accounting system capable of meeting government contracting requirements?	

Capability and Capacity

Here's where you match your business' capabilities with the demands of government contracts:

Task	Description	Completed (Yes/No)
Assess Internal Capabilities	Do you have the necessary skills, experience, and resources to fulfill contract requirements?	
Plan for Equipment/Staff	Do you have access to the necessary equipment and staff, or plans to acquire them?	
Subcontractor Agreements	If needed, have you identified and vetted potential subcontractors?	

Proposal Writing and Negotiation Skills

Winning government contracts repeatedly is no small feat. It requires compelling proposals and sharp negotiation skills:

Task	Description	Completed (Yes/No)
Develop Proposal Writing Skills	Are you or your team equipped to write compelling government contract proposals?	
Understand Pricing	Do you know how to price your products/services competitively for government contracts?	
Practice Negotiation	Are you prepared to negotiate terms, prices, and deliverables with government agencies?	

33

Past Performance and References

Lastly, the government often considers a business' past performance and references in awarding contracts:

Task	Description	Completed (Yes/No)
Compile Past Performance	Do you (or your subcontractors) have a list of past projects that showcase your reliability and quality?	
Gather References	Can you provide references from past clients, particularly for similar work that can vouch for you?	

Summary

These checklists are your starting blocks in the race for government contracts. Ticking off the boxes doesn't guarantee you'll win a contract. If you're unsure about taking the leap, the checklists help assess your readiness. The assessment may highlight areas you didn't consider. Remember, government contracting can be a rewarding field, and preparation is key. Use these checklists as your guide, fill in those gaps, and get your business in prime shape to tackle government opportunities.

Manifest
Inc.

Please scan the QR code for more insight. If you would like to further the conversation, feel free to reach out via Facebook, Instagram, or schedule a call via our "Lean on Me" service.

Chapter 7

COMMON MISTAKES IN GOVCON

In the maze of GovCon, there are common mistakes small businesses make when stepping into the federal marketplace. But don't worry, I'm here to help you sidestep those pitfalls, so you can march confidently towards your first (or next) government contract.

The Pitfalls
1) Not Having a Solid Business Foundation

The Misstep: Would you build a house on sand. Not the best idea, right? Well, diving into GovCon without a solid business foundation is pretty much the same. Some companies jump at the opportunity without legally transforming their interest (or hobby) into a business (sole proprietorship, company, or corporation). This shaky foundation can lead to disastrous results when faced with the rigorous demands of government contracts such as delays and denials. Having a legally formed business, clear financial records, and a good understanding of your own operational capabilities goes a long way.

The Dodge: Before you even think about bidding, ensure your house is in order.

-Ensure your company is formed with your Secretary of State's Office (county or city for sole proprietorship) and if applicable set up a Doing Business As (DBA) naming structure.

-Have a clear understanding of your business' financial status. This includes cash flow, expenses, and debts.

-Be honest about your operational capabilities. Can you really deliver what you're promising, on time and to specification? If not, consider partnering with someone who can.

2) Assuming the Government Doesn't Buy What You Sell

The Misstep: "Oh, the government won't be interested in what I have." Ever said that before? It's a common misconception among small businessowners. The truth is, there are over 400 federal government agencies, and they buy a wide array of products and services, from paper clips to rocket ships. Assuming they don't need what you offer is a missed opportunity.

The Dodge: Do your homework. Government agencies might be one of the largest customers you could have. Here's how to align your offerings:

-Use resources like the Federal Procurement Data System (FPDS) and USASpending to see what the government has been buying. Be sure to search by your NAICS code.

-Attend government-hosted industry days and networking events to learn about upcoming federal government requirements and trends.

-See what businesses are selling similar products/services to the government. If agencies are buying from them, why wouldn't they buy from you?

3) Not Being an Expert in Your Industry

The Misstep: If you think you can wing it, think again. Government agencies contract with businesses that can confidently claim expertise in their field. If you're not up to date with the latest trends, technologies, or regulations in your industry, you're starting at a disadvantage.

The Dodge: Be the expert, or at least, hire one.

-Remain abreast of industry trends, technologies, and best practices. Never stop learning.

-Obtain relevant industry certifications and make sure they're current.

-Through marketing, thought leadership (like blogging or speaking at conferences), and successful past performance, make it clear you're a an expert in your field.

The Importance of a Solid Business Foundation

Your business is like a tree. Without strong roots, the tree won't stand tall, and it might topple over during strong winds. Challenges in contracting present those strong winds. A solid foundation allows for easier access to resources. Understanding your financial position, reducing risks, increasing credibility, and preparing for growth support a resilient structure that can handle the unique pressures of government work.

-Risk Reduction: A well-structured business can better manage risks associated with government contracts, such as payment delays or stringent compliance requirements.

-Increased Credibility: Demonstrating a solid foundation increases your credibility with government agencies. They're looking for reliable, stable partners, not hobbyist.

-Growth and Scalability: With a solid base, you're better positioned to scale your operations up or down based on contract demands.

The Importance of Knowing the Government Market

Ignorance isn't bliss in GovCon. Assuming federal agencies won't buy what you sell removes opportunities to gain new customers. Gaining market knowledge broadens opportunities, increases strategic positioning, and informs business decisions. The government could very well be the most lucrative customer you're NOT selling to.

-Broadened Opportunities: Understanding the government market opens up new avenues for business growth and diversification. Who knows, you may be able to launch a new product or service based on a government need.

-Strategic Positioning: By knowing what the government buys, you can tailor your offerings and marketing efforts to meet their future needs, placing you steps ahead of competitors.

-Informed Business Decisions: Market knowledge contributes to sound business decisions, helping you invest in the right areas and avoid wasting resources.

The Importance of Being an Industry Expert

In the vast sea of contractors, being recognized as an expert in your field is a lighthouse guiding government clients to your shore. Flaunting your knowledge is alright, but make sure you can deliver. Agencies are paying for your knowledge and expertise.

-Competitive Advantage: Expertise sets you apart in the competitive bidding process, making your proposals more compelling and credible.

-Quality Assurance: Breath and depth in industry knowledge shows you're more likely to deliver high-quality products or services, leading to better performance evaluations and future contract opportunities.

-Adaptability and Innovation: Experts are better equipped to adapt to industry changes and innovate, keeping their services relevant and in demand by the government.

Summary

That's the lowdown on some common pitfalls and ways to "dodge" them. Remember, building a solid business foundation, recognizing the government's vast market potential, and proving yourself as an industry expert are beneficial steps on the path to success. Keep these points in mind, and you'll not only avoid common mistakes, you'll also position your business as a strong contender in the GovCon arena.

Chapter 8
PREPARE TO LAUNCH

You want to do a systems check before launching. There's a few considerations to make before liftoff. No worries, your guide is below, so strap in, and prepare for launch!

Step 1: Complete Your Business Setup
Make sure your business is in operational shape. This includes having a clear business structure, up-to-date finances, and a solid business plan. Ensure all your licenses and insurances are current and that you're all set legally to provide services or products.

Step 2: Register and Certify
If you haven't already, complete your registration in the System for Award Management (SAM). Without this, you can't bid on federal contracts. Also, if you qualify for any small business certifications (like 8(a), HUBZone, WOSB, VOSB/SDVOSB), get with a specialist at SBA to find out more. Small business certifications offer valuable contracting opportunities through set-aside programs.

Step 3: Brush Up on GovCon Basics
Before you even draft your first proposal, ensure you understand the basics of GovCon. This means knowing a little about the FAR (at least where to find it), understanding how solicitations work, and getting familiar with the types of contracts out there. Consider online courses, webinars, or local workshops to build your foundational knowledge. SBA and APEX offer free courses, and they partner with other organizations to offer free courses as well.

Step 4: Research and Network
Start by identifying potential government customers who might need

what you offer. Attend industry days, matchmaking events, and other networking opportunities hosted by government agencies or industry groups. Building relationships can be key to getting your foot in the door.

Step 5: Find Opportunities

Use government databases like SAM to find open solicitations that fit your business' products or services. Understand how to read solicitations and note the ones that align with your capabilities and capacity.

Step 6: Develop Your Proposal-Writing Skills

Writing proposals for federal government solicitations is a mix of art and science. Take the time to learn how to craft compelling, compliant, and competitive proposals. Consider taking specialized courses to improve your skills in this area or hiring professionals with experience.

Step 7: Price Your Products or Services Correctly

Understanding how to price your offer is crucial. Your pricing must be competitive. At the same time you must ensure you cover costs and make a profit. Research pricing benchmarks for your industry, develop pricing strategies, and learn pricing requirements involved in government contracts (i.e. allowable and unallowable costs).

Step 8: Submit Your First Offer

Once you've found a solicitation that's a good fit, and you've prepared a strong proposal, it's time to submit your offer. Follow all instructions carefully, double-check your work, and send it before the deadline.

Step 9: Get Your Tools Ready

Equip your business with the right tools and resources. This includes industry-specific software, project management tools, a skilled workforce, and anything else that will help you fulfill government contracts efficiently.

Step 10: Learn from the Process

Whether you win or lose your first few offers, there's always something to learn. Analyze feedback from unsuccessful offers and use it to improve future proposals. Always request a debriefing from the Contracting Officer. Please submit your request within 3 days after you receive notification of contract award, or no more than 3 days after you find out the contract has been awarded (whichever comes first). Celebrate wins. Also, review what worked well so you can replicate your successes.

Step 11: Stay Persistent and Adaptable

Government contracting is a marathon, not a sprint. Stay persistent, keep bidding, and be willing to adapt your strategies based on your experiences and industry changes.

Step 12: Plan for Growth and Scalability

As your experience in GovCon grows, start planning for the future. Consider how you can scale your operations, expand into new markets, or leverage past performance into new opportunities.

Summary

It's a wrap! From getting your business in order and registering in SAM to finding opportunities and submitting offerors, you now have the roadmap to succeed.

You've learned the importance of networking, pricing your products or services competitively, and understanding the federal contracting process. But most importantly, you've seen that GovCon is a long game—it takes planning, persistence, and adaptability.

Now take everything you've learned, apply it, stay the course, and start building your future in government contracting. Here's to your success in the GovCon arena—may your launches be smooth and your landings profitable!

Manifest Inc.

Please scan the QR code for more insight. If you would like to further the conversation, feel free to reach out via Facebook, Instagram, or schedule a call via our "Lean on Me" service.

Afterword

If you're feeling overwhelmed, don't worry—you're not alone. The transition from private to public can be a complex process, filled with new terminology, procedures, and regulations. Consider this book your foundational guide, the first step on your path to becoming a proficient government contractor.

Understanding the Basics

Before getting into available resources, let's recap the basics. Government contracting involves selling products or services to the government, which can range from local city contracts to large federal projects. In this book, we've primarily talked about the federal government; state and local government agencies are similar with a few differences. It's a market with its own set of rules, but also with significant opportunities for growth and stability for your business.

Educational Materials and Resources

For those new to GovCon, the learning curve can be steep, but there are plenty of resources designed to help you overcome it. The internet is a treasure trove of information, so it's essential to know where to dig.

Small Business Administration (SBA): The SBA offers a wealth of information specifically tailored for small businesses looking to enter the government market. Their website includes guides, tools, and training programs that cover the basics of GovCon, how to find contract opportunities, and how to bid competitively. DSBS, Dynamic Small Business Search is a tool used to lookup small businesses and obtain additional information about entities. Businesses are able to add their capabilities narratives, bond levels, performance history, etc. This additional information helps contracting professionals conduct market search.

System for Award Management (SAM): This platform is where you can find federal contracting opportunities. Familiarize yourself with this site, as it will become one of your primary resources for finding potential government projects.

Defense Logistics Agency (DLA): For businesses interested in defense contracts, the DLA provides webinars, training sessions, and other educational materials to help you understand the defense procurement process. DLA also manages DIBBS (DLA Internet Bid Board System). DIBBS is a web-based system that allows submission of quotes in response to posted RFQs. The system allows users to search and view RFPs and IFBs.

APEX Accelerators (formerly known as Procurement Technical Assistance Centers (PTACs)): APEX Accelerators offer one-on-one counseling, workshops, and seminars to help businesses understand and succeed in the government marketplace. They are an excellent resource for personalized support. Keep in mind, each center's capabilities are as good as the individuals that work in them.

Manifest, Inc.: That's us! At Manifest, Inc., we are dedicated to educating business owners on the GovCon process. We understand that every business' journey is unique, which is why we advertise and offer workshops, classes, and seminars covering a range of topics related to GovCon. Whether you're struggling with the basics or looking to refine your proposal writing skills, we're here to help guide you through every step of the process.

Professional Associations: Joining professional associations related to your industry and/or GovCon can provide networking opportunities, industry insights, and access to specialized training and seminars.

The Road Ahead
While this book serves as an introduction to government contracting, it's just the beginning of your journey. Recognizing the vastness of this field, we are committed to providing ongoing support and education through Manifest, Inc., and our upcoming series of books.

In our future works, we will delve deeper into specific areas of government contracting, such as pricing strategies, proposal writing, contract management, and compliance. These focused guides will build on the foundation laid by this book, offering you a comprehensive understanding of each aspect of government contracting.

Final Thoughts

Remember, the transition to government contracting doesn't happen overnight. It requires patience, persistence, and a willingness to learn. But with the right resources and support, it's a transition that can significantly benefit your business in the long run.

So, take advantage of the materials and organizations available to you, including Manifest, Inc. We're here to support your growth in this new area, offering clarity and guidance on your journey to becoming a successful government contractor.

As you close this book, it isn't the end, but the beginning of your exciting government contracting adventure. As a convenience, I've included blank pages for you to write down your thoughts and capture any notes or key pieces of information. We look forward to assisting you with your next steps and beyond. Welcome to the world of government contracting – your future awaits!

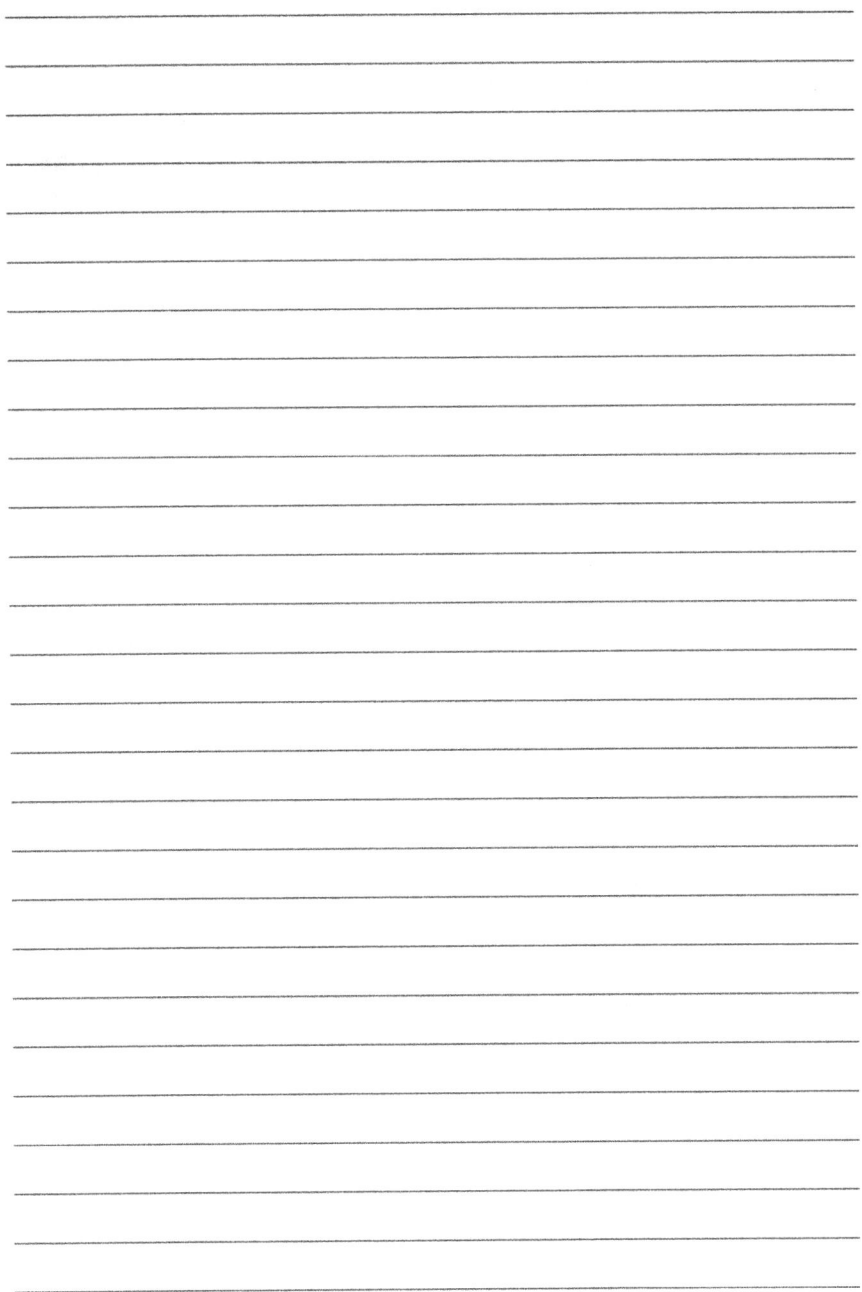

About the Author

Kesha Murry-Stowe is an accomplished expert in federal government contracting and an enthusiastic advocate for entrepreneurship and financial literacy. With over 15 years of experience, she has become a pivotal figure in guiding small businesses through the complexities of securing government contracts. Raised in Los Angeles, her firsthand encounters with urban poverty fueled her determination for economic empowerment and social mobility.

Kesha's professional journey includes serving as an Army officer and becoming a certified financial manager, which equipped her with a unique blend of skills she now shares through her nonprofit organization, Manifest Inc. There, she educates small business owners on the realities of government contracting, dispelling the misconception that it is a playing field only for large corporations.

In addition to her work with Manifest Inc., her educational initiatives also extend to the youth through the T.Y.P.E (Teaching Young People Entrepreneurship) program, where she teaches young entrepreneurs about the foundations of business management, helping them to craft vision and mission statements, select appropriate business models, and develop robust financial strategies.

In this book, Kesha shares her extensive knowledge and practical insights into government contracting, aiming to equip readers with the necessary tools to navigate this sector confidently and successfully. Her commitment to education and empowerment is reflected on every page, offering a roadmap for anyone looking to expand their business horizons and thrive in the competitive world of federal contracting.

Connect with the Author

To further enrich your experience, I invite you to connect with me through various platforms. Stay updated with the latest insights, tips, and exclusive content that complements the book by following these channels:

Facebook: Manifest Inc.
Instagram: @manifest_inc
Website: www.manifestme.org
YouTube: Manifest Inc.

Feel free to reach out with your questions, share your experiences, or engage in discussions about the topics covered in the book. Your journey in government contracting is important, and I'm excited to be a part of it. Together, we can explore the potential, dispel the myths, and uncover the opportunities that government contracting offers.

Thank you for your support and for choosing to connect. Let's make your government contracting journey a successful and rewarding one!

Warm regards,
Kesha L. Murry-Stowe
Author, Government Contracting Expert

www.ingramcontent.com/pod-product-compliance
Lightning Source LLC
Chambersburg PA
CBHW070902210326
41521CB00010B/2030